RY BERNDORFF
159 GLENFOREST RD.
TORONTO, ONT.
M4N 2A3

416 - 483 - 3978

CASA GUATEMALTECA

KATIA NIESIOLOWSKA

CASA GUATEMALTECA

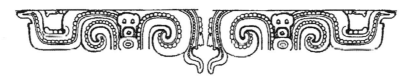

Director, designer and editor
BENJAMÍN VILLEGAS

Photography
ANGE A. BOURDA

Texts
JORGE LUJÁN MUÑOZ

Foreword
BENJAMÍN VILLEGAS

Villegas editores

This book has been created, produced and
published in Colombia by
BENJAMÍN VILLEGAS & ASOCIADOS
Avenida 82 No. 11-50, Interior 3
e-mail: villedi@cable.net.co
Telephone 616 1788. Fax 616 0020
Bogotá, D.C., Colombia.

© VILLEGAS EDITORES 1999
© KATIA NIESIOLOWSKA

www.villegaseditores.com

Layout
MERCEDES CEDEÑO

English translation
JIMMY WEISKOPF

First Edition
August, 1999

First reprint
August, 2000

ISBN
958-9393-71-3

The publisher wishes to express special thanks to
CEMENTOS PROGRESO S. A.
for sponsoring the first edition of this book.

Front cover: *A modern living room in a colonial setting.*
Back Cover: *Antigua garden.*
Pages 2-3: *Antigua Guatemala, calle del Arco, in the
 background La Merced church.*
Page 4: *Restoration of a colonial fountain.*
Pages 6-7: *A contemporary country house.*

Niesiolowska, Katia
 Casa guatemalteca / Katia Niesiolowska;
Director, designer and editor Benjamín
Villegas ; Photography Ange Bourda ; Text
Jorge Luján Muñoz; Traduction Jimmy
Weiskopf — Bogotá: Villegas, 1999.
 248 p.: ill..col.; 22.9 x 28.0 cm.

 Includes bibliography
 ISBN 958-9393-71-3

 1. Architecture domestique - Guatemala
 2. Architecture - Guatemala I. Tít. II.
Villegas, Benjamín, ed. III. Bourda, Ange, ill. IV.
Luján Muñoz, Jorge V. Weiskopf, Jimmy , tr.

 728 CDD
 NA776 LC

CONTENTS

FOREWORD

There can be no doubt that houses are the measure of man and in that sense a wager on life. You don't build a house so that it won't last, nor to fight with its inhabitants. Houses are destined to be a demonstration of human coherence. And it has always been that way, from the shelters first built at the dawn of humanity to contemporary styles of habitation – a history of epochs and styles in which the handling of space ranges from the austere to the exuberant.

The houses of Guatemala, shown in a representative sample in this book, are no exception to the above rule. The gracefulness with which they conserve and interweave architectural motifs inherited from their wealthy ancestors, the way they achieve harmony with a landscape that is privileged but unpredictably volcanic, the passion they display for contrasts of light and shade and for the vegetation that surrounds each space, the natural intuition evident in the sure selection of materials, all this confirms – if there were any doubt – that habitat reflects the individual.

And, when we enter these houses, the decorative repertoire further emphasizes the sense of life that unfolds there. Legacies, traces of the past, presences and imagination give sentiment and intimacy to these living spaces and a sense of continuity and re-encounter.

These Guatemalan houses seem to show how much a house is, in reality, an investment in love. Houses, urban or rural, which exhale a desire to recover the meaning of life, gardens which assert the right to repose, spaces which encourage reading and relaxation, dwellings of human dimension where the family may always find a refuge at the end of the day, when work is over.

With the approach of the new millennium these Guatemalan houses seem to provide conclusive proof that the house, as a habitational alternative, continues to be a valid solution, even though the contemporary mass-production world in which we live frequently tends to sidestep it.

Leaving aside matters of theory and analysis, a perusal of these houses leaves us with the certainty that the Guatemalan house, by virtue of its power of evocation and mysterious effect on our feelings, is unique and unrepeatable.

BENJAMÍN VILLEGAS

Opposite page: *Contemporary Antigua garden, with a restored colonial fountain which reproduces baroque forms and a path with clay floor tiles, seen from a restored house through a wrought iron grille.*

Above: *A colonial nativity scene in cedar wood with polychromatic finish and silver crowns.*

A large colonial building in Antigua that has not only been respected but also given additional elements such as the garden and fountain.

INTRODUCTION

KATIA NIESIOLOWSKA

The idea of doing a book about Guatemalan houses came to me after seeing the many books that are being published about houses in different parts of the world, books that show how the history, customs, art and folklore of the countries are reflected in the particular way that each culture has of organizing the most intimate space that man inhabits: his house.

Guatemala is a country with a privileged geography and a double ancestral culture. This culture has bequeathed to its people not only the impressive cities and monuments of the pre-Hispanic past, with their strong stone sculptures, polished ceramics, rich polychromatic textiles and exuberant sense of colour but also the Spanish heritage of architecture, woodwork, religious and lay goldwork…and also, of course, a certain sensibility. The Guatemalan house had to strongly reflect the integration of these historical currents, as well as the influences other peoples and cultures have left upon the country. Its culture and historical traits have been like a magnet which attracts and welcomes a wide variety of immigrants from Latin America and the rest of the world.

In fact, during the work that was done for this book it became evident that in many Guatemalan houses the past and the present - which are always projected towards the future - have managed to live together harmoniously on a pleasant human scale that does not clash with their surroundings. This is because in Guatemalan architecture, tradition is the common trunk out of which each generation has grown.

This book is a window onto many of those houses which still exude an aroma of authenticity through their walls, patios, rooftiles, bricks, fountains and *búcaros* (the typically Guatemalan recipient for the fountain´s water). Houses whose owners feel a profound love for their culture, their history and their roots. Majestic or simple houses, located in the most diverse regions of the country, built in a variety of tastes and styles but always attractive because of the interest they awaken in the visitor and because they leave us with the fascinating sensation of having entered into a reality that is so current yet so remote and, at the same time, so authentic and personal.

I would like to express my profound thanks to all those who gave me their support and trust by opening the doors of their houses to me and sharing part of their lives and memories. I would especially like to thank Benjamín Villegas, the publisher, Ange Bourda, the photographer and Enrique Novella Alvarado, without whose strong support and permanent encouragement this project would never have reached its fortunate conclusion.

Opposite page: *Detail of the stairway of a contemporary Antigua house which tries to create a colonial atmosphere within a modern space, the effect being heightened by the glazed tiles on the stairs and the successful selection of objects and furniture.*

Above: *Niche in the form of an aureole with an archangel carved in wood with a polychromatic finish.*

CASA GUATEMALTECA

JORGE LUJÁN MUÑOZ

Few cultural artefacts better reflect a society's values and way of life than its residential houses and the way they have been modified. The house shows us the traditions, origins, spirit, tastes, needs and preferences of a society, according to its different social strata.

It has been said that the best portrait of a nation may be found in its productive activities: agriculture, industry, trade. I think, however, that one of the most revealing ways of understanding a society is to study the evolution of its domestic architecture and the way in which it has arranged its living spaces.

The house has been defined as "a building to live in", a dwelling, a residence, a home. The way in which people live expresses their wants and luxuries, the objects they love and the intimacies of their domestic life. It shows not only the weight of history but also the influence of new trends, the economic, ideological, social or cultural differences among its classes and the penetration of foreign elements.

In residential architecture the permanent superposition of the past and future are clearly seen. Houses from past epochs are still in use, even though the people who now inhabit them are in every sense very different from those who built them.

Nowadays, for example, we speak of the colonial house in the present tense, but we must not forget that the society which produced it has disappeared and that those who now live in such homes have different customs, attitudes and needs. This why we have to install bathrooms with all the modern additions in them, hide televisions and cd players in old cupboards, put old-fashioned kitchens to new uses as we prepare foods with modern technology and so forth, all of which further transform the original house.

In many cases the Guatemalan colonial house and its offshoot, the republican one still serve as homes but they have been transformed in order to adapt to a different era in which people live in a different way.

Our country's house has a double origin, Spanish and indigenous. The former includes urban and rural colonial buildings, initially built for the Spanish population and later, for the creole and mestizo one. The latter is represented by the continuing tradition of the pre-Hispanic house and its food plot, an architecture found in Indian villages in colonial times and maintained, with some modifications, up to the present day. We should not forget, of course, that many indigenous settlements adopted Spanish architec-

Opposite page: *Exterior of the garden of a restored Antigua house, which conserves the original stone walls.*

Above: *Colonial sculpture in cedar wood.*

tural elements which became part of the traditional domestic architecture of the country on a local level.

This essay is meant to serve as a general historical introduction that complements the photographs found in this book, which illustrate the exteriors and, above all, the interiors of a sampling of present-day Guatemalan houses.

To better explain their appearance and contents we have decided to lead the reader in a journey, however superficial, through the history of Guatemalan domestic architecture and its furnishings. We must warn the reader, however, about the difficulty of distinguishing architectural tendencies or movements in our country, for which reason, I have tried, as far as possible, to avoid being very specific about such matters. I am convinced that the person who looks at these photos, reads their captions and goes through this introductory text, will have a very good opportunity to capture the meaning and value of the subject of this book.

Above: *A living room which successfully combines different kinds of furniture with colonial objects and paintings.*

Opposite page: *Corridor of a contemporary house in Antigua which incorporates arches with a mixture of curved and straight lines widely used in Guatemala during the last stage of the baroque, clay floor tiles and doors with turned wood balusters.*

Historical evolution is a permanent process of tension and communication between the spirit and meaning of the previous epoch and the new ones that are coming into being. This process leaves its mark on architectural spaces. It shapes the origin of influences—the models or archetypes; the evolution of tastes and uncertainties, preferences and rejections; the play of search and encounter. I believe that the houses in this book are a good example of the preferences of a certain sector of Guatemalan society today, people who seek to live in distinguished and comfortable homes and, at the same time, appreciate and surround themselves with high-quality national and foreign art.

The Colonial house

The domestic urban architecture of Guatemala, like that of most Latin American countries, derives from the Spanish model predominant in Andalusia—which, in turn, has a Roman origin, with some modifications which came from the Arabs—although with different proportions, since in

general, the Latin American house is larger and its rooms and patios occupy a bigger surface area.

The most common arrangement was that of a main door with an entrance hall that gave onto the central or first patio, an inner courtyard which had a rectangular form and four equal galleries, one on each side. In smaller houses this patio was smaller and only had two galleries. The sitting or reception room faced the street and was found on the most convenient side of the entrance hall. The two lateral galleries housed the bedrooms and other living spaces used by the family, like the office or study, sewing room and so forth. At the far end of the two lateral galleries one entered the service patio, where the kitchen, pantry, laundry and servants' quarters were found. The larger houses had an area at the back called the *corral,* where there was a chicken coop and a garden as well a place to keep carriages and horses. Access to this area was also to be had through an independent or service entrance located on the same street as the main entrance or on a side street.

Because of the danger of earthquakes the Guatemalan house generally had one or, at the most, two storeys and very thick walls. No examples of colonial houses with more than two floors are known.

An important part of the urban Guatemalan house was the portal, located in the centre of the façade. The surviving examples, almost all from the seventeenth and especially, the eighteenth century, surround the doorway and extend out from the façade of the building.

The best ones have stone jambs and lintels and were wide enough to allow a carriage to pass through them.

A revealing example is the portal of the so-called "Casa de los Leones" or "House of the Lions" in Antigua Guatemala, where elements from various epochs are superimposed. The stone jambs and pilasters are carved into a pattern of entwined plants, which might come from the sixteenth or early seventeenth century. The lintel, otherwise very plain, has a split pediment above it, probably from the seventeenth century. The Solomonic columns,

Opposite page: *Small interior patio of a restored house in Antigua, with a view of the old kitchen with a fireplace in the form of a cupola and access through a door with small turned balusters.*

Above: *Bedroom of a house in Antigua, with a modern wrought iron bed and canopy.*

Main living room of a house in Antigua, incorporated into the original vaulted space, with bare brick and stone walls. It is decorated with contemporary furniture and colonial paintings and sculptures.

22

which are very characteristic of the late seventeenth or early eighteenth centuries, seem alien to the building and may have originally been part of another one. Verle Annis guessed that they might be from the nearby Santa Catalina monastery. It is probable that the lions, which are now on top of the Solomonic columns, were once found on a second floor, since they are, by all appearances, heraldic figures.

The patios were flanked by galleries with slightly sloped roofs, called Spanish terraces, for the fall of water which was at times through gargoyles. Usually, these terraces were supported by wooden columns on stone bases, although there were also brick ones. The width of the galleries was between three, four or even five *varas,* a Spanish measurement roughly equivalent to a yard, though the popular *vara* could be either longer or shorter.

Above: *Contemporary fountain with its* búcaro, *which incorporates traditional baroque forms.*

Opposite page: *Stone-paved entrance hall and partial view of the patio of what was the Colegio Tridentino in Santiago de Guatemala, the present-day Antigua. It was designed by the Chief Master Builder Bernardo Ramírez, around 1750, with mixtilinear arches.*

When the houses had offices or shops attached to them that belonged to the owner, these had separate street entrances, although they were internally connected. All of the rooms had a door onto the galleries but they were also connected to one another so that one might, if necessary, walk from one bedroom or other living space to another without having to go out to the gallery. In corner houses the sitting or main living room was located on the corner and usually had a right-angled window with a column in its apex. In the patios, which did not have a garden as they do now, and in certain parts of the galleries or other heavily transited areas, the floor was usually of flagstones, while in the bedrooms it was made of terracotta bricks of diverse forms. In the most important areas, like the chapels, the bricks were complemented by glazed tiles, which were also used in the window ledges, some fountains and *búcaros* and the bathrooms that were not far from the main patio.

In a few houses there were bay windows, generally on the second floor, for the use of the ladies and other members of the owner's family.

Other important elements worth mentioning in the Guatemalan urban colonial house were the use of tiled roofs over *par y nudillo* trusses over the

bedrooms and the previously mentioned "Spanish" terraced roofs covering the galleries.

Raised lanterns or gables were placed in some bedrooms, and in the kitchens there were room-sized chimneys which had a similar volu metric and masonry treatment. In the kitchen area, it was not unusual to find ovens for baking bread within the house itself.

The building of fountains was a characteristic feature of Guatemalan houses, apparently from a very early period. They were placed in the centre of the first patio, with stuccoed or stone basins. In the secondary patios, they were placed against or embedded into the wall, which probably derives from renaissance or mannerist styles, since similar ones are frequently found in the Italian architecture of those periods and were perhaps the original models. In Santiago de Guatemala, there were many of these fountains which consisted of a half basin of stone or plaster into which flowed the water which gushed forth from the mouths of diverse ornamental figures or faces, at times of saints like Santiago. These ornamental fountains were known earlier by the name of *búcaros*, which is still used today. In the second or third patio, the laundry basins were found with an area for hanging clothes out to dry.

The windows on the exterior façades were roughly twice as high as they were wide and had ledges above which wooden balusters, originally and later, iron grilles, were usually placed to protect the windows.

While the floor plans of the houses were not modified to reflect the new artistic standards, now known as baroque, that became predominant between the second half of the seventeenth and the first seventy years of the eighteenth centuries, various important innovations were made in details. The portals, which no aristocratic residence did without and were occasionally made of stone, received varied decorative touches, including carved figures. The corner windows were maintained and the Solomonic order was incorporated into their apex columns, while very simple pilasters were always used in the corner doors. Windows of all kinds, above all those which

Opposite page: *Old Antigua fountain in the rear patio of a restored house. The fountain was originally used to wash clothes.*

Above: *Detail of a washbasin in the bathroom of a house near the lake of Amatitlán, decorated with glazed tiles, and a skylight in which rustic wooden beams may be observed. The floor of clay tiles is inlaid with glazed tiles.*

27

Above: *Dining room of a contemporary house in the city of Guatemala, with pieces of Antigua majolica on the wall; in the background, a plaster colonial sculpture in the corridor.*

Opposite page: *A sitting room joined to the patio with its pool and furnished with Mexican leather chairs.*

were found in the inner patios, were modified through the introduction of new upper end profiles of an hexagonal, octagonal or lobulated type. The use of glazed tiles increased, both in fountains and *búcaros* and in zocles, kitchens, window ledges and other places. The arches in the entrance halls and in the service area had lobulated shapes with a mixture of curved and straight lines and and even conopial contours. The height of some houses was also increased and more elaboration was given to the decorative details of the kitchen fireplaces, the raised lanterns or skylights and the crownings of the spiral staircases. Nor should we forget the so called "pleasure patios", which had undulating flowerbeds. Everywhere the taste for the curved, predominant during the baroque, was revived.

In Nueva Guatemala, where the neo-classical was fashionable, there were no fundamental changes in the traditional arrangement of the rooms of the houses of prestige, which were all located on the blocks near the main plaza. Changes were limited to details in the portal and some features, like columns and pilasters, which incorporated the reduced repertory of the classical order and the use of stone. Houses continued to be of one storey because of the fear of earthquakes, which limited architectural possibilities, in contrast with the seigniorial houses of the cities of México or Puebla, in Mexico, where, in the eighteenth century, the number of storeys was increased and ample and bold arches were made in the spaces containing the staircases. In Santiago de Guatemala, now La Antigua, there were a few exceptions to this rule, among which the so-called Casa de Chamorro or de Llerena stands out, a two storey house with a simple stairway, attributed to Luis Díez Navarro.

During the nineteenth century the colonial house was little changed, maintaining more or less the same division of spaces, although an increase in land values led to the subdivision of properties, reducing the size of houses and their rooms. The most common model was that which subdivided the large house with a big patio and four galleries into houses with

two galleries and a central patio that became progessively smaller.

The domestic architecture mentioned up to now corresponds to the central part of the great Spanish and creole cities, where the most important families lived and shared their dwellings (respecting class barriers, of course) with relatives, servants of various races and some black or mulatto slaves. The members of the family and their relatives lived around the first patio, while the indigenous and mestizo servants and the black slaves had their sleeping quarters at the back of the building. The urban houses of the middle classes were smaller, with more reduced patios and fewer galleries, as has already been mentioned. By contrast, little is known about how the lower strata of the urban population lived. For example, what is today conserved of Antigua Guatemala is, almost exclusively, the inner city, where the residences of the most powerful families were found. Only in the surroundings of La Merced and what was the parish of San Sebastián do a few small colonial houses survive, some of which are mentioned by Verle L. Annis in *The architecture of Antigua Guatemala 1543-1773*. In any case, the poor neighbourhoods near Santiago, where the houses of the less favoured classes were found, no longer exist.

We may assume that in other urban centres of the *Reino de Guatemala* (the Kingdom of Guatemala) houses of different kinds were built, but probably without so much contrast, since the important ones, though they did have two patios and a similar distribution of spaces, were not as big as those of the capital. Christopher H. Lutz argues that the Indian settlements where there was a certain socio-economic stratification among the native inhabitants themselves had some houses, with several rooms and outbuildings, that were the property of wealthy indigenous families. This author mentions several Indian villages in which there were some Spanish and mestizo families which must have introduced their domestic architecture, among them Quetzaltenango, Chimaltenango, Almolonga (Ciudad Vieja), San Martín Jilotepeque, Sololá, Santa Cruz del Quiché, Huehuetenango, San Marcos,

Opposite page: *Detail of the corridor of a present-day Antigua house decorated with indigenous masks, rattles and large clay pots.*

Above: *Interior of a contemporary house in the city of Guatemala. The arch relates the living room to the dining room, which combines colonial figures, indigenous ceramic pieces and modern objects of art.*

Opposite page: *Open gallery facing the fountain patio on the second storey of a house in Antigua, with a wood board floor and a combination of Guatemalan and Indonesian objects and textiles.*

Above: *Part of the old kitchen of the house, with the segmental arch of the fireplace decorated with majolica plates, an old table in the foreground, and, in the background, on top of the old stove, a group of objects and figures of saints arranged in the manner of popular altars.*

Escuintla, Petapa, Amatitlán, Mixco, Zacapa and Guazacapán, to which we could add, in a later period, Totonicapán, San Cristóbal Totonicapán, Patzicía, Patzún, San Juan Sacatepéquez, Sacapulas, Cobán, San Pedro Carchá and some others.

In almost all of these towns there probably lived wealthy indigenous families which might have had houses that were at least similar to those of the Spaniards and mestizos of a middling economic position, although not as large nor with such a complex structure as those of Santiago de Guatemala. We should not forget that the ethnic composition of those who lived in such houses was homogenous, since all were members of the same indigenous family.

Lutz does not agree with the general belief, which overly simplifies the nature of the indigenous

Above: *Dining room, with indigenous masks and paintings by Miguel García Luque, in the city of Guatemala. Several pieces of furniture are combined with a Solomonic column and colonial sculptures and paintings.*

Opposite page: *Contemporary house in the city of Guatemala. There is a work by Claude Le Boul above the door, a picture by Joaquín Vaquero above the fireplace and, to the right, works by Armando Morales, Humberto Garavito and Elmar Renè Rojas. The atmosphere is adorned by a rich variety of orchids.*

dwelling during the colony and claims that it was a very rustic, single-roomed hut or shack, that is, what is known today as a *rancho*, built with four posts, a straw or palm-leaf roof, wooden poles, mud and cane walls, or at times, adobe. In the colonial period the náhuatl word *jacal* was used. In his opinion, indigenous houses showed variations of size, shape and style, the same as those of the Spaniards, creoles and mestizos. For reasons of climate, materials and local tradition, it is evident that there were regional differences. The use of roof tiles, wooden windows and doors, portals, ovens and the rest was adopted, at least for certain rooms.

In other words, the cases in which the indigenous dwelling incorporated popular Spanish elements and had an internal arrangement of several rooms around an earth patio were not very infrequent, while at the same time they continued to employ motifs and solutions of a pre-Hispanic kind, among which the use of the steam bath or *temascal* in the high plains region stands out.

Some old hacienda houses are also conserved. These are a type of brick dwelling with a tiled roof and a portal supported on wooden pillars. The simpler houses had two or three pillars; the larger ones enlarged the

gallery, which was faced by the bedrooms and other domestic rooms. In some nineteenth century engravings one may see hammocks in these galleries.

As was pointed out in the introduction, an important part of a residential house are the furnishings and there is no doubt that these varied according to the social class of its inhabitants. In fact, furniture was as much or even more of a distinguishing feature of the house than the architecture itself. We have already seen that the houses of the elite were bigger and more complex, with a reception room, separate bedrooms for different members of the family, places of work and relaxation, dining room, kitchen and other areas. Each of these rooms had well-defined furnishings, which were gradually renewed as novelties arrived from Spain and were adapted

to Guatemala. These included chairs, armchairs, carpets or reed mats and pictures, among other objects in the reception room; and beds, chests, large chests, some kind of wardrobe, tables, chairs and similar things in the bedrooms. It was also customary to build cupboards into the walls, with or without doors. In the bedrooms it was usual to have paintings or sculptures of the saints of personal devotion. Nevertheless in the more "distinguished".houses it was not unusual to find a domestic oratory or chapel, with a main altar at one end and lesser one at the sides, praying chairs, pieces of gold work, etc. Nor should we forget the objects used for illumination: table or standing candelabra, hanging lamps and others, as well as drapery, cabinets and musical instruments. The clavichord was very popular at one time and later, the piano.

When the houses were more modest the rooms were reduced in size and number, or were even limited to one or two which served for all purposes. The furniture was less ostentatious, not renewed so frequently and therefore not so "fashionable". Instead of carpets they used mats of *sibaque* fibre and there were no paintings of quality or originals, but at most engravings or coloured prints.

Opposite page: *Gallery of a contemporary house in the capital, with large windows in the background. On the table and the walls there are carved, polychrome colonial statues.*

Above: *Large sitting room, dominated by a fireplace with a carved relief and various pieces of antique furniture and statuary that stand out against the rustic walls with their traditional whitewash.*

The Republican house

After independence, urban domestic architecture did not change except for a greater emphasis on classical tendencies, in particular those of French origin, above all in the repertory of decorative elements. In the city of Guatemala the tendency to build the most important houses near the main plaza or major convents was maintained.

In his book of memoirs, the Guatemalan writer Antonio Batres Jáuregui (1847-1929) includes a description of the houses of the city of Guatemala at the end of the nineteenth century worth quoting:

"The houses were of one storey... All the houses had large patios, in case of earthquakes, and were whitewashed with lime both inside and out, which was hygienic but not very aesthetic. There were no carpets, only mats of reed or petate textiles. The ceilings were, at times, of whitewashed blankets that moved in the wind. The furnishings consisted of: a round table in the middle of the hall, a large sofa, several chairs matted with reeds or upholstered with untreated horsehide, some religious paintings and the portraits of the ancestors of the owner of the house; some white curtains of a cheap fabric to cover the window; a little brazier with embers to light cigars; some old sculptures of saints or perhaps a glass globe covering the Holy Wafer. The floor of the galleries and the bedrooms was of rough earthen bricks. The spacious entrance hall was adorned with cow backbones embedded in the floor in primitive patterns and in the centre the date on which the house had been built was marked with such bones; around the entrance hall there were mortar benches used as seats by those who arrived and in one of the corners you detected the foul-smelling visitor's urinal, placed there to avoid the need of running a long distance to the innermost part of the house in cases of urgency. The street doors were monumental, studded with bronze rosette forged nails; the bulky knocker, in the form of a lion or a dog, hung from the main door. At night the entrance was weakly illuminated by a tallow candle lit within a lamp. Inside, the sitting rooms had lamps of crude petroleum, which was called gas, despite being liquid. The patio, which was quite big, was rustically paved."

Other details are mentioned by José Milla (1822-1882), who, in a sketch of local customs published in 1881, includes a precious and revealing

Above: *Colonial window with its whitewashed frame against the deep red wall, an oil painting by Deborah Duflon to the left and other pieces of rustic furniture.*

Opposite page: *Bedroom of a restored house in Antigua which combines different colours and forms: the white wall, the earth-red of the fireplace with coconut-shell masks placed on it, the indigenous textile in which the red and brown of the "cuyuscate" (cotton) predominate and a chamula hat from Chiapas.*

paraxgraph about street windows, especially those of the sitting room and the role which they played in social life over a century ago. It shows us how much customs have changed and how the function of these windows (which led to so many romances and the founding of so many families) has disappeared:

"The windows! There indeed is the most interesting part of a house from many points of view. I won't bother mentioning that they help to provide a good part of the ten cubic metres of air which, according to physiologists, are needed by an adult man enclosed within his room. I will only speak of the important role which this oblong opening made in the outer wall of the house and equipped with an iron grille and some window panes is destined to represent in the life of those who inhabit that urban district. The girls prefer the window to any other part of the house. What would they do without them? Our wary grandfathers

furnished the windows with thick shutters, a word [celosías, similar to "distrustful"in Spanish] which betrays the unhappy origin of those apparatuses which the girls of the present generation would declare abominable. Nowadays the windows are frank and open. From five p.m. onwards (especially on Sundays and holidays) the young and feminine part of the family takes possession of them: they are their means of communication with the outside world. Later on, at night, the windows often play an important role. Oh, if those grilles that adorn them could speak! But I mustn't be less discrete than the crude metal of which they are made".

The houses described in the above texts refer, as should be obvious, to those in the capital which belonged to the well-off. From other sources it is possible to get an idea of what those in some rural areas were like. The English traveller Henry Dunn, who was in Guatemala in 1827-1828, refers to the domestic architecture of Gualán, Zacapa, where most houses only had two rooms, separated by a light wooden partition. In one of these rooms, says Dunn, the whole group of travellers he stayed with ate and slept. There were five small beds there, a large wooden table, some chairs of the same material, two hammocks which permanently hung across the room and three or four swords and several muskets which "adorned" the wall. Shortly after

Opposite page: *A statue of the Holy Father dominates the atmosphere of this living room of a restored house in Antigua, whose segmental arch with exposed brickwork integrates the two spaces, decorated with rustic and modern furnishings, colonial sculptures and silver objects.*

Above: *Traditional kitchen with its typical poyo or cooking range, fireholes, fireplace and firewood, which contrast with the blue of the pewter pots.*

In this Antigua living room, which we can see through the segmental arch with exposed brickwork, there are various colonial sculptures and objects. The first is a Virgin with a silver crown standing on a large wooden capital. In the background, where the whitewashed masonry is combined with part of the old wall, there are other sculptures and above the fireplace, whose mantelpiece is decorated with silver objects, a painting of an archangel and to the right, a traditional wardrobe. The modern sofas with white upholstery have cushions covered with indigenous fabrics in which red and purple predominate.

42

the travellers arrived several local people visited the house, which was always open. One got into a hammock, while others sat at the table or on the beds and began to ask for the latest news and to argue vehemently about politics while they smoked and spit profusely onto the floor.

The American traveller, George Washington Montgomery, who visited Central America in 1838, also offers some interesting details about rural houses in the narrative of his visit. He describes the one inhabited by the *Comandante* of the port of Trujillo, in Honduras, located in the fort. It was a single large room, made up of four walls without any partitions, without a ceiling and with exposed roof beams. On one side there was a door that gave onto the street and on the opposite one a smaller door that gave onto the patio of the fort. The floor was of brick with

Above: *Terrace roof, converted into a social area, with a view of the tiled roofs and other buildings of Antigua.*

Opposite page: *Old patio transformed into a garden. The vegetation offers protection from the sun and the rain while at the same giving a new meaning to the life of the traditional house.*

some palm-leaf mats. This room served for everything except cooking: it was the sitting room, bedroom, dining room and office. It had a comfortable sofa, a good cedar table to eat on, a bed and a desk. The bed was a metal one, raised, on a platform, some sixty centimetres above the floor and had the inevitable mosquito net above it.

The same Montgomery describes the house of the parish priest of Zacapa, near the church. It had a portal, an interior patio, and although it was large, he did not consider it comfortable. As well as the sitting room it had two other rooms, one of which was the bedroom of the priest. He regarded the furnishings as being of a "classical simplicity". In the sitting room, placed against the wall, there was a wooden bench with a back and arms and a large *caoba*-wood table, all arranged as though in a court. Against the walls there were a dozen chairs with leather seats and backs fastened with nails. Facing a picture of Christ there was one of the Virgin Mary.

The same Dunn makes a passing reference to the furniture which he saw in an "elegant" house in the city of Guatemala. In the sitting room there were ten or a dozen old chairs; a no longer fashionable sofa; a mat which served as a rug; two small dressing tables, placed at a considerable

distance from each other, each with the picture of a saint in a glass globe; three or four paintings on the white-washed walls; and two silver lamps that hung from the roof. In other rooms he mentions having seen a *caoba* wardrobe and a sideboard with glass doors which housed china and porcelain. In the dining room there were only a large oak table and seven or eight wooden chairs. Nearby was the kitchen, where his attention was drawn to the oval oven in one of the corners and the *poyo*, a stone or masonry platform that served as a cooking range and in this case was about three or four feet high and had six or seven openings for cooking fires.

Next to the kitchen was situated the patio with its basin, stables and an additional trough for the use of animals.

Throughout the nineteenth century, some urban and stylistic processes took place which were reflected in residential houses. Renaissance and romantic trends led to the incorporation of ornamental details, although the rest of architecture did not vary. The creation of gardens became fashionable. One of its expressions was the conversion of the paved urban plazas into what were now named "parks", which were planted with a variety of trees and flowers: the most important was the "central park" in the old main plaza. Another was the building of masonry flower beds in the patios of private houses, where ornamental plants were sown, although the fountains and paving were still maintained. Another transformation was the elimination of eaves, which were replaced by cornices. There was also the arrival of cement, which little by little passed from public to domestic architecture, with the aim of making buildings safer and speeding up their construction. By the same token, glass roofs were incorporated, whether in skylights or in parts of the patios and galleries.

Beyond this, there were some examples of prefabricated houses imported from other countries, especially the United States and particularly California, which at that time was the most accessible supplier through steamship and railway connections. Around 1846, the French traveller and natu-

Opposite page: *Living room of a country house in San Pedro in which folkloric touches are combined with antique furnishings within a contemporary structure.*

Above: *Bedroom of a restored house in Antigua, with a bed and a mosquito net above it.*

ralist Arturo Morelet wrote that imports of "furniture and luxury objects" from Europe had recently increased, their clients doubtless being the wealthy families of the capital. Following the prosperity brought by coffee in the last quarter of the century, this process became accentuated to the point where a good part of domestic furnishing were imported, in particular suites for the sitting room, dining room and kitchen. In some cases, "frenchifying" meant that most of the interior decoration of the house came from France - the furnishing of the sitting rooms, the curtains, the carpets, the pianos, the paintings, the tableware and other household goods.

Some foreign estate owners began the fashion of building country houses, following the rural architecture of their respective nations. In some cases they bought prefabri-

Above: *A picturesque and eclectic kitchen-dining room in a small contemporary house in the city of Guatemala. There is a big picture by the painter Jose Antonio Fernandez above the dining table.*

Opposite page: *Circular stairway rising from a marble floor of black and white squares in a contemporary house in the city of Guatemala.*

cated houses, in others they had them built in Guatemala, but they always tried to copy the models of the respective "mother country". There were German families that not only imported spouses for their male and female children but also all of the furnishings and articles for their homes and, of course, elegant clothing for special occasions. In photographs taken by Edward Muybridge in 1875, examples of this kind are already found, almost all of them belonging to first-generation foreigners. This leads us to suppose that the process actually began some decades before, becoming more accentuated later on and also influencing urban architecture.

In general there was, then, a loss of traditional elements, a process which led to the "de-nationalization" of the house, which became ever more foreign-looking. Even paintings, landscapes and still lifes which had nothing to do with the country were imported. Nor was it unusual for these prosperous entrepreneurs to commission oil portaits from some second- or third-rate European painter when they travelled abroad.

A separate mention is required for the late nineteenth and early twentieth century buildings of Quetzaltenango, where an architecture with European roots was developed, done in stone and based, above all, on classical

models: it is found both in public buildings and ostentatious family homes. This influence spread from there to other towns in western Guatemala and the tradition lasted well into the twentieth century.

The new domestic architecture

In architecture, as in other aspects of the country's life, earthquakes have played a decisive role in Guatemalan history and those of December 1917 and January 1918 were especially important. In the capital architectural trends which had begun to arise before these earthquakes took on a new strength during the work of reconstruction that followed them. Among them were the building of chalet-type houses, the importing of prefabricated ones, especially of wood, and the use of zinc roofing sheets. A variety of imported models were used for the building of chalets, which strengthened the influence of foreign architecture.

Many of the new houses in the historic centre of the city were built on subdivided properties. This produced a narrowing of the entrance halls to more or less half of their original size and a reduction in the size of patios. The spread of the automobile caused more streets to be paved. Garages were built into both inner-city and suburban houses, either by remodelling the entrance hall or by specifically building an independent entrance for cars.

Some houses that were built around this time had touches of the *art nouveau* style, a trend—mostly limited to details in the façade, entablature or window grilles—that did not transform the basic distribution of spaces in the interior.

The rebuilding of the city of Guatemala was slow, a delay aggravated in part by internal political problems but mainly by the effects of the world economic crisis of 1929-1930. In those years the first apartment buildings, based on U.S. models, were built. More or less around the decade of the thirties began the "neo-colonial" or what one critic has called the "neo-vernacular" fashion, both in public buildings and, above all, residential houses. Ideas were taken from recent Mexican and Californian models and this style

Opposite page: *Bedroom of a restored Antigua house, with the original bare masonry walls and wrought iron bed.*

Above: *Contemporary sitting room of a house in the capital; above the fireplace, a picture by the Nicaraguan painter Armando Morales.*

Estate house of a coffee farm on the outskirts of the city of Antigua. This type of house is characteristic of many other farms of the region: a single storey, a central enclosed garden, a tiled roof, long galleries with corridors opening onto the interior space, in this case a pretty garden with a lawn and flowers. The windows of the bedrooms open onto the plantations.

Above: *Main façade of contemporary mansion in the city of Guatemala, designed by the architect Carlos Ramírez.*

Opposite page: *Vestibule of a contemporary house, with a circular stairway, wrought iron railing and bronze chandelier.*

was employed, above all, in chalets. This trend was characterized by the use of Spanish roof tiles, a proliferation of arches, skylight-type windows, decoration with helicoidal columns and other elements of colonial architecture. At the same time the art deco style and the first stage of the so-called "international" one arrived, which were incorporated into both public buildings and private homes. That is, from 1920 onwards a new architectural phenomenon was seen in the country - a heterogeneity of styles and influences. The architect Robert Hoegg, trained in Germany, kept himself apart from the neo-colonial school, designing highly functional buildings and houses which had straight lines, a great horizontality and nothing of ornamentation.

Despite these neo-colonial expressions, we do not find a "nationalist" current, particularly in domestic architecture, that is, a style based on local roots that seeks an authentic character. This was probably the result of the ideologies of the ruling classes but it also had to do with the absence of Guatemalan architects. Most of the builders in the country lacked professional training in architecture and, with very few exceptions, the small number of professional architects in Guatemala were recent descendants of foreign families, like Juan Domergue, Roberto Hoegg, Francisco Cirici and Manuel Moreno. One exception was Enrique Pérez de León, trained as an architect in France, who in his personal works, but not in his government commissions, was influenced by international tendencies.

In these years there were interesting architectural experiments in Mexico and Brazil which found no echo in the country. In addition, government architecture in the period of Jorge Ubico was influenced by the dictator's taste for anachronistic styles, which halted the penetration of art deco and the international school. Nationalist currents were also absent from interior design. The works of living Guatemalan artists and local popular arts were still scorned. With a few exceptions, wealthy families did not buy works by Guatemalan painters, and even less did they give them prominence in their

homes or offices or collect archaeological or historical pieces. This is why the interior of their houses had an undefined atmosphere, without "personality" or national character. Guatemalan painters and sculptors found it difficult to sell their works. The artistic taste of the wealthy classes was backward, preferring a "realism" that was already very distant from the best contemporary European or American art. The trends in Mexican plastic art reached certain artistic circles but did not touch the educated public in general. All of this meant that the Guatemalan house of this period had little character or authenticity. Instead, there was a copying of foreign tastes that were already outdated.

The Guatemalan house of the past half century

From 1945 onwards important political, social, economic and cultural changes took place in Guatemala which had an effect on architecture in general and housing in particular. For one thing, the country began to open itself up to *avant garde* currents in art, which led to a general improvement in taste. At the same time a number of professional architects who had been trained abroad, mainly in the United States and Mexico, returned to the country: they not only assumed a new role in Guatemalan architecture but they also helped found the country's first faculty of architecture, which was inaugurated in the Universidad de San Carlos in 1960. The graduates of this faculty stimulated the search for an architecture that would be in harmony with the predominant world tendencies and at the same time offer adequate solutions to their own cultural tradition and the environmental conditions of their country.

The growth of economic prosperity and the emergence of a new class of the educated and prosperous increased the demand both for residential homes and low-income housing projects. To begin with, there was hardly any construction of apartment buildings: single-family houses in the new suburbs, especially those of the capital, predominated. The taste for the so-called neo-colonial style remained, but there also began to appear houses

Opposite page: *Vacation house designed by the architect José Asturias on a steep hillside near Santa Catarina Pinula, with a view over the valley of the city of Guatemala. It is an octahedron with large triangles which open and close electrically.*

Above: *View of the octahedron when it is closed by the electrical device.*

Above: *Interior of the second floor of a vacation house on the banks of the river Tatín, Izabal, designed by John Heaton in the style of a hut thatched with corozo-palm leaves.*

Opposite page: *Exterior of the same vacation house, built in the local indigenous style, using traditional techniques and materials.*

that were inspired by the most recent "international" currents, as well as ones in a less defined "eclectic" style.

Guatemalan domestic architecture also showed evidences of the plastic integration which had been seen in public architecture since the middle of the nineteen fifties. Of course, the experiments were on a minor scale. But in a few houses reliefs, mosaics, murals and other decorative features by national artists were used both in exteriors and interiors.

The homes of the wealthy also changed with the emergence of professional interior decorators, a new appreciation for national contemporary plastic art and the "discovery" of popular crafts and pre-Hispanic and colonial arts. These elements were now seen to give character and elegance to the decoration and adornment of houses. In a matter of years, Guatemalan artists received a new recognition, both in an economic and an aesthetic sense: their prices rose and their works were prominently displayed in bourgeois homes and offices.

While what we have said about the evolution of the house in Guatemala applies to the capital and its adjoining districts, it also includes vacation houses, most of them the property of residents of the capital, and some houses belonging to the owners of country estates. Weekend or vacation houses and chalets began to appear about fifty or sixty years ago, first in Amatitlán lake, and later in places like the beaches of the Pacific, Antigua Guatemala, Atitlán lake and río Dulce and on farms, rural lots and other places. These vacation houses showed the same tendencies as those of domestic architecture of the capital and had a similar interior decoration. In lake and beach districts picture windows were installed in order to enjoy a view of the landscape from the inside of the haven provided by the comfortable interior spaces. Designs—rustic, sophisticated, modern, etc.—varied according to the climate, local conditions and personal tastes and some have been very successful.

A case apart are the houses in the historic centre of Antigua Guatemala. Credit for the "discovery" of this city as a vacation home goes to a

number of Americans who restored or rebuilt houses that had been found in different stages of abandonment or deterioration, converting them into comfortable and highly atmospheric residences. Perhaps the first example, at the end of the nineteen twenties, was the house of Doctor Wilson Popenoe, an ample corner residence which was restored with good taste and dedication. Others are that of Mrs. Mildred Palmer (1936-1940), who, with a sure hand, restored a small corner house behind the old cathedral which she named the Casa de las Campanas, using the colonial name of that street; and that of Mrs. Matilda G. Gray, another large corner house which she later expanded by including neighbouring properties which are used as gardens. These houses inspired other foreigners and Guatemalans who were not from Antigua to follow the same pat-

tern of buying and restoring traditional houses. The results have varied but their owners have respected the current architectural regulations for the conservation of the city, which has been officially declared a "Monument of America and Heritage of Humanity". Their example was also followed by some wealthy residents of Antigua, who were interested in converting their houses in the historic centre into agreeable domestic spaces that respect the urban setting. Both in architecture and decoration, they have sought to give these houses an atmosphere with a colonial "stamp" that respects their historical flavour and is, at the same time, pleasant to live in.

Conclusions

The houses chosen for this book show the happy combination of circumstances which have contributed, in the past three or four decades, to the improvement of the exterior and interior quality of Guatemalan architecture. One of these is the emergence of a generation of architects who have a good professional level, are really up to date in their work and are interested in finding solutions suitable for the country and its traditions. Another is the way in which those who are able to pay for the best architecture,

Opposite page: *House in the city of Guatemala built shortly after the earthquakes of 1917-1918 with reinforced concrete, which allows for some slender pilasters that, joined to the high roofs, give it an airy feeling.*

Above: *In the patio of the same house, a marble sculpture similar to those which were imported in 1897 to embellish the Paseo de La Reforma. Both the cement floor and the balustrades facing the patio which adorn the roof were very fashionable during the first half of this century.*

Large social area of a contemporary residence in the city of Guatemala, designed by the architect Peter Giesemann, with different connected levels and spaces. The floor is of black slabs from South Africa. The right line predominates and there is a simple design, with white roofs and walls which highlight the many paintings: to the left, a red abstract painting by the Guatemalan artist Moisés Barros; in the centre, over the fireplace, a picture by the Ecuadorian painter Hernán Cogollo, and, to the right, one by the Mexican artist Roberto Cortázar.

whether urban or recreational, have broadened their artistic tastes. They have developed a genuine interest both in contemporary national arts, whether cultured or popular, and traditional ones that range from the archaeological to the colonial and the republican. They understand how to gracefully incorporate these objects into the atmosphere of their rooms. Finally, we cannot forget the contribution of the artists and craftsmen of the country, whose works, backed by a long tradition, have played a critical role in creating the bold and happy combination of architecture and decoration seen in the houses shown here.

Their variety and quality has been achieved within a broad range of styles. After seeing all the examples which are illustrated here–a necessarily brief selection–we have no choice but to admire and be

Above: *Living room of a vacation house on Lake Atitlán, with a tiled floor and a picture by María Dolores Castellanos.*

Opposite page: *Entrance to a contemporary vacation house on the shores of Lake Amatitlán, with old doors incorporated into it.*

Pages 66-67: *View over the colonial city, from the terrace roof of a restored Antigua house.*

pleased with the results. It is a good sign that Guatemalan architects and artists of the most varied tendencies are valued today; that cultured and popular art and our historical heritage are appreciated; and that home-owners are working together with professional architects and designers to build houses that are, as never before, pleasant, modern, original, comfortable and faithful to our own traditions.

The modern Guatemalan house is very different from the traditional one. This is why traditional elements as important as the entrance hall and galleries have almost completely disappeared from its daily vocabulary and why the street windows which were so gracefully described by Pepe Milla no longer have an important social function, at least in the suburban houses of the capital. Daily family life today is different and the same applies to its architectural solutions.

I would like to finish by pointing out an interesting contrast. While the country is full of buildings that are imported copies or imitations, without local character or originality, it is reassuring to know that there do exist Guatemalan houses which combine tradition and modernity to create pleasant surroundings that have a flavour of their own.

Garden which embellishes and lends colour to the stone ruins which were incorporated into a restored house in Antigua. The fountain and the walls seen here are in their original, somewhat destroyed state, probably because of the 1917 earthquake.

Above: *Old stone façade above the garden which surrounds a restored house in the city of Antigua.*

Opposite page: *Gallery which constitutes the main entrance to the same house, where the colonial columns and other original elements that the restoration, by Amerigo Giracca, took advantage of can be seen, as well as the fountain and the living area in the background.*

Above: *Details of the same
house in Antigua in which one
may appreciate the use of the
clay floor tiles, colonial-style
furniture, varied ornaments and
the original walls which show
their patina and the passage of
time. In the background, the
contemporary stairway built into
the wall, with a wrought iron
railing.*

Opposite page: *To the right,
the stairway, seen from another
angle, connects the different areas
of the house, within a vaulted
space. In the foreground there are
several artisana wood
candlesticks with a silver patina
and in the background, a small
corner lounge decorated with
cushions in typical Guatemalan
textiles.*

Bedroom of the same house,
restored in Antigua by the
engineer Amerigo Giracca and
adapted to a vaulted interior
space, with very simple furnishing.

74

Another bedroom of the house in Antigua, with wrought iron beds made by local craftsmen. The whole structure is new but stuccowork has been employed in

certain areas, like the surroundings of the arch, to lend a traditional atmosphere.

Pages 76-77: *Circular fountain in the entrance patio of a restored house within stone ruins in the city of Antigua.*

The *Agua Volcano*, the
dominant element in the Antigua
landscape, transmits its elegance
and serenity to the interior
garden of this traditional house.

78

Opposite page: *Portico that forms the entrance to the interior patio-garden of a traditional Antigua house.*

Above: *Gallery with clay floor tiles, flanked by wooden columns resting on hammered stone, seen through a colonial arch of adobe and stone.*

Bedroom of a restored Antigua
house, with a contemporary
fireplace adapted to the space,
which connects with a small
sitting room through a door in
the thick colonial wall. The cross
seen in the background, above
the red wood stretcher, is also
colonial.

Living room of a house in
Antigua which combines
traditional furniture, a restored
fireplace with a statue of
Santiago on horseback and two
European paintings on each side
and a large Chinese Coromandel
screen. To the left, a colonial
religious picture above a
Venetian bureau.

Pages 84-85: Old colonial
kitchen transformed into a
dining room and decorated with
diverse iron objects, masks,
lamps with wooden bases and
bronze pots.

Above and opposite page:
Entrance to a contemporary house in Antigua and side view through the garden. Here traditional architecture is combined with an ample green zone which takes advantage of the stone remains of colonial buildings, destroyed in the 1773 earthquake, found amidst the vegetation.
Beside the house, a wide paved driveway for vehicles and a fountain surrounded by bougainvilleas.

Main living room of a present-day house in Antigua with walls painted in a light yellow, a modern fireplace above which there is an oil painting by the contemporary Guatemalan artist José Luis Alvarez and on either side two paintings by unknown artists, one of Santa Rosa de Lima adoring the Virgin and the other of a figure with a nude torso, between two baroque reliefs.

Small contemporary living room where we can see, on the wall on the left, a space designed to display a collection of pre-Hispanic stone axes from the Maya culture. Above the fireplace, pieces of Antigua majolica and Mayan vessels.

At the end of a long corridor
opening onto the garden, this
small living space is decorated
with a dhurry *from India in
soft colours. A group of rustic
chairs, which form a lounge area
and two eighteenth century wood
sculptures complement the corner.
In the background, near the old
bare masonry wall composed of
different kinds of stone, there is
a large carved wooden altarpiece.*

Above: *Traditional bedroom of a house in Antigua, decorated with carved doors on the wall and colonial columns at the sides of the beds.*

Opposite page: *Detail of the traditional Guatemalan carved cedar wood doors, hung above the antique table which displays Mexican ceramic objects.*

Opposite page: *Large Antigua garden, designed around the remains of colonial buildings destroyed in an 18th century earthquake.*

Above: *Colonial fountain of whitewashed stone, with a* búcaro, *in Antigua. Behind, the cupola of the colonial kitchen of the original house.*

Living room of an Antigua house opening onto an inner patio, with a floor which combines clay and glazed tiles. Over the fireplace, there is a primitive wooden sculpture of an angel and two local Majolica plates and on either side of it, modern wrought iron candlesticks. In front of the fireplace there is an inlaid wooden chest with a geometrical design, an example of traditional Antigua craftsmanship.

Bedroom of a house in Antigua
which blends furniture from
different periods, popular ceramic
objects, a painting of Antigua
and six silkscreen pictures by the
artist David Ordóñez, which

hang between the mirrored doors.
The setting is dominated by the
chromatic strength of the
contemporary Mayan textiles
used in the cushions and
bedspreads.

Another bedroom of the same house, with a similar decorative concept, where both the walls and furniture are full of small colonial, popular and fine-art sculptures, among them various twentieth century crucifixes and masks. The bedspread and the cushions are of indigenous Guatemalan textiles.

Opposite page and above: Two views of the same living space in an Antigua house, restored by the Guatemalan engineer Amerigo Giracca. They are of an old kitchen which conserves its cupola-shaped brick fireplace. The restoration retains its old smoke patina and the kitchen has been adapted to its new use as a living room, with traditional and modern furniture, a shelf with antique pharmacist's jars and a framed, bright-red Mayan huipil *textile*.

In this study-library of a contemporary house in Antigua, the built-in bookshelves seen in the background are combined with an antique writing table and a carved sideboard. Beneath the large segmental arch with exposed brickwork, which contrasts with the terracotta floor tiles, there is a colonial sculpture in waxed cedar.

Stone-paved interior patio of the same house, with stone steps which contrast with the clay floor tiles. In the background, an old door which gives access to the sitting room. To the right a niche with a gilded colonial sculpture beneath which there is a rustic pine table from Nahualá (Sololá) with various silver objects; to the left, a Spanish-style chair and beside it, a painting by the Guatemalan artist Marco Augusto Quiroa, above an antique carved chest.

Reconstructed Antigua house. In
the foreground, a gallery with
traditional floor tiles and plants.
To the left of the grassy patio, a
gallery with wrought iron crosses
on the wall. On the right side
and in the background, some
typical colonial lobulated
windows have been reproduced.

104

Passage of a contemporary house in Antigua where an interesting atmosphere has been created with a hemispherical vault with exposed bricks. On the left wall, eight indigenous masks used in traditional dances; to the right, a platform with a popular polychrome sculpture of an archangel.

Opposite page: *View of the main cloister of the former Colegio or Seminario Tridentino, designed by the Chief Master Builder Bernardo Ramírez in the middle of the eighteenth century and now a private home. It recalls the patio of the colegios menores of Salamanca, with thick columns of mixtilinear arches.*

Above: *The graceful main portal, which combines typical elements of the high baroque in Santiago de Guatemala: columns covered with small pilasters between which are stone ashlared pilasters; on the entablature diverse examples of period ornamentation; and above, a niche framed by scrolls and small pilasters inside of which is the Virgin of the Assumption in mortar.*

Above: *Another view of the
cloister of the former Colegio
Tridentino, Antigua, converted
now into a private home. The
flowerbeds are a modern addition.*

Opposite page: *The Spanish-
style dining room of the house,
where a fireplace has been
incorporated and decorated with
Antigua majolica plates.*

Opposite page: *An Antigua patio, with a stone fountain embedded into the wall beneath the shade of the trees, facing the residential part of the house.*

Above: *Main entrance of the house with a grille of modern design. The passage, which leads to the patio, is decorated with a large primitive wooden relief, above a rustic table.*

Sitting room decorated by the designer John Heaton, with a multicoloured variety of oriental textiles placed on the armchairs and the sofa. Over the stone fireplace pieces of Mexican pottery, Mayan vessels and an antique archangel stand out against the strong orange wall. A Venetian blown-glass chandelier hangs from the wooden roof. On the wall on the right side there is a picture by the Mexican painter María Ruibalbo.

Bedroom of the same Antigua
house, with a fireplace decorated
with inlaid glazed tiles and
crowned by a mirror with a
gilded aureole. To the left, the
primitive wooden wardrobe which
is complemented by the
indigenous woven rug. An ikat
textile from Indonesia hangs on
the wall.

Above: *Passage leading to the dining room of the house, with hand-painted vault. The indigo of the wall serves as a background for the two popular ceramic pots with flowers, two wooden columns and a Marian sculpture, without gilding, in the centre.*

Opposite page: *The dining room of the house, painted a strong orange, is decorated with a popular crucifix and an altarpiece pilaster which has lost its gilding; the window and door are highlighted by their indigo frames, as is the popular wooden sculpture by its white niche. The table is made of an old carved door.*

Opposite page: *View of an area in the process of reconstruction, part of which is a garden, which belongs to an eighteenth century Antigua house that was destroyed by an earthquake. We can observe the original walls that lead into a room.*

Above: *Pool built among the ruins, joined to the side garden by a colonial stone wall. In the background, the cupolas of the colonial city.*

A small living room in Antigua, beneath a cupola, with polychromatic walls and seats made of concrete with cushions on them. A Roman arch provides access to it from the main living room of the house, which is of contemporary design within an old structure.

118

Entrance to the dining room of
a house in Antigua, which is
preceded by a niche in the bare
stone and brick wall. It has a
contemporary firework whose

polychrome has been applied by
hand and whose opening is a
stone arch. The floor mixes clay
and glazed tiles.

119

Above: *Dining room, within a restored area, of a house in Antigua. The walls have been stuccoed and their corners rounded. The contemporary glass table is surrounded by Spanish-type chairs. To the right, a colonial painting and a*

Solomonic column in carved wood. In the background, a sideboard with gilded reliefs that displays two colonial statues of acolytes in wood with a polychrome finish. In the centre, a reproduction round colonial mirror.

Opposite page: *Part of an Antigua house, which has been restored in the form of a chapel, with a vaulted brick roof, altar in carved polychrome wood and column bases used for indirect lighting.*

Opposite page: *An Antigua house restored at the beginning of the twentieth century, with a floor of cement paving stones, classical circular wooden columns resting on stone bases and popular furniture.*

Above: *Bedroom with a bed with a carved wooden polychrome headboard. The contemporary rug is hand-made and has jasper motifs. The bedspread is an indigenous textile. The base of the shuttered window has been turned into a window seat.*

Opposite page: *Contemporary Antigua house in a colonial style, with original antique architectural elements, such as the carved stone arch built into* *the entrance of the dining room and the bases of the windows.*

Above: *U-shaped interior gallery which surrounds the patio and provides access to all of the rooms, furnished with clay amphorae and colonial furniture.*

Dining room of the previous house. In the centre, above a contemporary table, hangs a wood and wrought iron chandelier. In the background, two niches with carved wooden statues and, on the left, a colonial liturgical chasuble placed above the side table. The floor is of terracotta tiles and old carved wooden doors have been incorporated into the structure.

Living room of the house, with a colonial chest and a large rococo mirror in the background. Behind the door frame built of old stone, there is a Guatemalan gilded baroque statue of the Virgin standing on a gilded pedestal and, to the right, within the living room, a wooden sculpture of the Virgin with Child, with a polychrome finish. A silver colonial lamp hangs from the roof. There are some candlesticks and a censer, also of silver, on the table.

Main bedroom with a bed that
has carved wooden columns.
The colonial chest, inlaid with
geometrical motifs, three colonial
oil paintings and a hammered
silver lectern also stand out.
To the right of the fireplace,
which incorporates parts of
the original stone, there is a
carved wooden Italian lamp
in the form of two children.

129

Above: *Contemporary kitchen lined with colonial-style glazed tiles, with rustic wooden furnishings and ceramics of the colonial period, from the firm of Montiel in Antigua, on the wall in the background.*

Opposite page: *Entrance, through an incorporated colonial stone arch, to the office, which has a beautiful bookcase in carved wood. In the foreground, a Virgin of the Conception in carved wood, with a polychrome finish and silver aureole, standing on a colonial cabinet.*

Corner dining room built into the patio of a restored house in Antigua, with a wrought iron table and Mexican pig-leather chairs. To the right, a rustic Nahualá table with bronze candlesticks. The floor is made of clay tiles of the region and displays a number of popular Guatemalan animal sculptures carved in wood.

At the back of this patio, a contemporary fountain done in a traditional style and lined with glazed tiles. It is surrounded by a garden onto which the galleries of the house open. To the right, a niche with a plaster aureole which displays a small carved wooden sculpture of an archangel with a polychrome finish.

Main living room of restored
house in Antigua, centred round
the fireplace, with a
contemporary, baroque-style
mirror. In the background,
carved wooden shelves which
display pieces of pre-Columbian
Mayan ceramics.

Master bedroom with a tapestry
bedspread and headboard and
cushions covered with folkloric
Guatemalan textiles.
In the background, antique
framed huipiles and a worked
tin mirror. Beside them,
primitivist paintings and
manufactured lamps that utilize
wooden angels as a support.

Opposite page: *A house in Antigua converted into an inn, designed by Mary Sue Morris, with windows that have wrought iron balusters that look out onto the stone-paved entrance patio. At the side of the door, brass lanterns.*

Above: *Old front door of the house, seen from the street.*

Bedroom of the house: the two
bedsteads of wrought iron have
bedspreads of a traditional
Guatemalan fabric, made of
pieces that have been joined by
hand-embroidery. The lamps are
of Mexican ceramic and a
sibaque *mat covers the floor.*

Bedroom of the same house with
clay floor tiles and a
contemporary fireplace in the
corner. The beds have a wrought
iron headboard and are covered
by Guatemalan textiles with a
jasper motif.

Opposite page and above: *Small sitting room that opens onto a gallery flanked by a longitudinal pool, parallel to the back wall, with water spouts and flowers in the niches. The furniture consists of rustic chairs* *with cushions covered by textiles and small tables in the form of a drum. The picture above shows the length of the pool, the traditional columns of logs and the rustic stone wall in the background.*

Opposite page: *View of an authentic colonial house in Antigua, adjacent to the Monastery of the Capuchin Nuns (behind the main part of the temple), that was probably built at the same time as the monastic building for the chaplain and confessor of the nuns.*

Above: *A corner of the patio, which shows the same type of cylindrical columns that are found in the cloisters of the convent and the semi-circular arches. At the end of the gallery one can see the arch that leads to the other rooms of the house.*

Interior patio of the same colonial house in Antigua, recently restored by John Heaton, which conserves the original fountain. This part of the house is partly reconstructed but it has conserved the essence of the original Guatemalan architecture of the period.

Opposite page: *Stone-paved entrance of a house in Antigua, seen through an arch. One can see the patio-garden, the steps that lead up to the gallery and the cylindrical columns with their traditional supports.*

Above: *Dining room of the same restored house, with a built-in fireplace, clay floor tiles and early-twentieth century furniture. On the left, a large wooden wardrobe and various wrought iron candleholders; in* the background, a side table with a gilded mirror; the table is set with pieces of Antigua majolica and two Fecho ceramic candlesticks, beneath a wood and iron chandelier with candles.

Bedroom of a house in Antigua. The white of the walls, rug and bedspread predominate. Touches of colour are lent by indigenous fabrics, one framed and the other used to cover an armchair, as well as the chest and painted candlesticks in the form of angels. The furnishing is completed by two locally-made, traditional small chairs and a rustic table with a majolica flowerpot from Totonicapán. The window ledges are decorated with Antigua glazed tiles.

Sitting room and library of the same house in Antigua. The furnishing and decoration are highly varied but form an agreeable whole. To the left, a monumental carved gilded mirror above the sideboard, *flanked by contemporary wrought iron candelabra. In the background, a bookcase with a central display case which holds Mayan pieces and colonial sculptures. To the right, a large colonial oil painting.*

Spacious garden of a contemporary house in Antigua Guatemala that serves as a complement to a colonial structure and utilizes traditional building elements like the tiled roof, exterior galleries and types of window. The garden displays a wide variety of vegetation which takes advantage of the climate and the possibilities offered by the valley of Panchoy.

Above: *A modern house within the framework of the city of Antigua. In a spacious site a beautiful garden has been combined with contemporary architecture which incorporates colonial stone ruins. It has a small modern fountain decorated with a sun in relief, a* búcaro *in local majolica and remains of the original structure that have been preserved and are partly covered by a bougainvillea.*

Opposite page: *Living room of the same house, which opens onto the garden through a large glass window. The interior, in light tones, is very luminous. The bookshelves with Mayan pieces, the clay floor tiles and the contemporary furnishings complement the atmosphere.*

Wall of the large sitting room of the previous Antigua house. The straight line, white colour and square spaces predominate; in the niches, where the zapote-fruit *colour combines with the floor tiling, pre-Hispanic objects and a colonial wooden sculpture with a polychrome finish are displayed. In the foreground, a table made* *out of an old door, with an interesting tin candelabrum of ten arms. Above the fireplace, two works by the Guatemalan painter Roberto González Goyri.*

154

Large living room in white and terracotta tones. There are various colonial pieces in wood, like the carved chest next to the white sofa, the rectangular table that divides the area, the corner table with a colonial silver lectern and two carved doors on the far wall, framing a painting by the Cuban artist Oscar Magnan. To their left, two small temperas by the Guatemalan artist Carlos Mérida and, beside the window, an oil painting by Irma Luján, another Guatemalan painter.

Breakfast room and kitchen of
the same house. The predilection
for the right line and light colours
continues, which is also found in
the folkloric tablecloth, with
Mexican ceramic tableware. On
the wall to the left, an
arrangement of Antigua painted
ceramic fruits.

Dining room of the same house. Once again, the play of planes in the square niches, this time with a yellow background, in which are displayed objects of art (Antigua and Spanish majolica plates and a popular sculpture) and a fireplace that is the same as the one in the living room.

In the centre, the table with a typical light tablecloth and glass and majolica plates, as well as napkin holders of painted hummingbirds, examples of the new local popular craftswork. The rug of pita fibre and cotton was made in Antigua.

House in Cobán, Alta Verapaz. Above, a bedroom in which white predominates both in the walls and the curtains, furniture, rug and bed. The latter, with canopy, has a bedspread with embroidered coloured flowers, as does the curtain. To the right, a view of the gallery of a Cobán house, with the typical floor of cement bricks from the beginning of the twentieth century, which combines well with the light orange colour of the wall and the furniture in cane and wood, which are often used in open galleries. The pictures on the wall are popular paintings, especially from the village of Comalapa, which are mixed with bronze stirrups.

Dining room of the same house in Cobán, with a European atmosphere and a small living room in the background. Both the table and the sideboard were made by local carpenters. The chandelier is of rock crystal and the wooden floor is covered by a large antique Persian rug.

Main bedroom of the house in Cobán, with an upholstered headboard and a baroque wooden carving that is set against the green background of the wall.

Opposite page: *A house in Cobán now converted into La Posada Hotel. To the left, the long gallery facing the garden, with the floor of big terracotta tiles, columns resting on octagonal bases of painted cement and simple rustic furniture along the gallery.*

Above: *In the bedrooms, the decoration contrasts the colour of the walls with those of the bedspreads and the rug, an example of the woollen craftwork done in the region of Momostenango, Totonicapán, which is repeated in the decorations on the red wall in the background. The base of the table lamp is a painted wooden horse made by the craftsmen of the region.*

Opposite page: *Restored house in Antigua which follows the traditional proportions and distribution of spaces. The corridor, adapted to contemporary ideas of a furnished gallery, leads towards a patio converted into a garden. The cane furniture is made in Cobán by local artisans. The door is of carved wood in the traditional style. In the background, a niche with a crown in the form of an aureole.*

Above: *Fountain in carved stone embedded in the boundary wall and approached by flagstones set into the garden.*

Spacious dining room with
intercalated clay and small
glazed tiles, in the same restored
house in Antigua.
 Its dimensions, the white colour

of the walls and the roof beams
give it an austere character. In
the background, above the
fireplace, a large archangel in a
wooden relief with a polychrome

finish, facing a small sitting
area. To the right, a gilded
baroque mirror and a carved
wood console table.

166

Main living room of the same
house. In the background a
colonial oil painting of San José.
To the right, an antique wooden
writing desk; on the wall a

European tapestry and a
large wooden sculpture with a
silver aureole. On the floor
there are colonial stone
column bases used as tables.

The panelled ceiling gives
warmth and character
to the space.

Opposite page: *To the left, within the same Antigua house, a corridor with exposed brickwork and an arched opening that leads to the kitchen, which is decorated with Antigua glazed tile and simple furniture placed on a floor of coloured cement.*

Above: *a spacious bedroom whose layout is dominated by the marriage bed, which stands against a large recessed arch whose border is decorated with volutes of carved wood left without finish or colouring. The pale yellow of the walls combines with the bedspread and the contemporary Antigua rugs. In front of the bed there is a folkloric bench on which there are several glass and porcelain pharmacist's jars.*

This living room with large windows of a house in the city of Guatemala opens onto a pretty garden. Varied elements are combined here: modern armchairs, traditional chairs, rustic wooden tables, oriental rugs, wooden beams and a bronze chandelier. On top of the tables there is a similar variety of objects: modern wooden lamps carved into the form of a fruit bowl, silver objects, ceramic ashtrays, a Christ Child sitting on the mantelpiece, a silver candlestick and a painting by the Spanish artist Miguel García Luque.

Bedroom of the same house in the city of Guatemala, in which warm colours predominate. The bed, which has a Guatemalan textile cover and kilim *cushions*, has a semi-circular wooden headboard, flanked by two reliefs carved into the shape of flower bowls. To the right, a portrait done by the Guatemalan painter, Ramón Banus, and on the wall behind the bed, two oil paintings by the Spanish artist, Miguel García Luque. A tin chandelier hangs from the ceiling and the wooden floor boards are covered with oriental rugs.

Vestibule that leads to the dining room, with colonial plaster statues of saints, a mirror with a fretwork frame and on the side wall, colonial volutes in carved

wood. In the dining room in the background we can see the stone bases of the table, a Solomonic column, paintings by Miguel García Luque and several

statues of the Christ Child on the wall.

Pages 174-175: *Spacious garden of a house in Antigua with a colonial-style fountain.*

Above: *Main patio of a restored house in Antigua that respects the traditional architecture. Note the waxed clay tiling, the wooden columns and capitals, the quetzal-tail plants which hang in the traditional way and the stone fountain in the patio.*

Opposite page: *To the right, one of the interior patios of the same house, in this case, stone-paved. The traditional building techniques are evident in the beams of the "Spanish terrace" roofs and the use of roof tiles.*

Opposite page: *Two living rooms connected by a carved double-door. There is a clay tile floor and a panelled wooden ceiling. The chairs and small tables are of the traditional Spanish type; on the left, note the bronze brazier on the rug. In the foreground, a wooden sculpture without a polychromatic finish of San José holding the Christ Child. On either side of the door there are landscapes in oil by the Guatemalan painter Humberto Garavito. In the room at the back, one can see a built-in cupboard with several examples of pre-Hispanic ceramics, including some polychromatic Mayan cups and to the right, a portait of an indigenous woman by another Guatemalan painter, Alfredo Gálvez Suárez.*

Above: *Another living room of the same house in which modern and antique furniture are combined; on the tables and the mantelpiece there are several silver objects; on the walls there are examples of colonial painting; and in the centre, a Virgen del Carmen with an extraordinary baroque frame.*

A more complete view of the
room shown on page 178.
On the right there is a carved
wooden wardrobe and on the left,
a colonial console. On the modern
glass-top table in the centre which
rests on gilded carved wooden
bases there are some interesting
examples of small colonial
Guatemalan sculptures. A
colonial silver lamp hangs from
the panelled ceiling. Above the
door in the background hangs
an old embroidered textile and
above the wardrobe, a piece
of colonial velvet.

Another view of the living room
shown on page 179. We can see
various kinds of republican
chairs and armchairs, wooden
tables from different periods with
silver candlesticks, as well as an
inlaid Spanish wood chest.

There are several colonial
paintings on the wall in the
background and the closed
shutters of a corner window or
balcony, an architectural solution
common to the whole of Central
America.

Above: *In the foreground, two niches with a backing of glazed tiles, displaying examples of local majolica; on the floor there are various types of terracotta Spanish amphorae and large jars used for the export of oil and wine. The arched door, which has a frame worked in* ataurique *(an Arab vegetal ornamentation), leads to the dining room.*

Opposite page: *Large dining room with simple wooden furnishing, including a table, sideboard and chairs with leather seats. The floor combines clay and small glazed tiles. Note the shutters of the windows, which have an interesting grooved woodwork, the mirror above the sideboard and the decorated ceiling. At the back, a framed colonial liturgical chasuble hangs between the carved doors.*

The kitchen of the house, joined to the breakfast room by means of an arch. In the foreground, a rustic table, with chairs, on which there are two candlesticks of

Antigua majolica and gilded wooden gourds on an oriental fabric. Behind the segmental arch, one can see the restored kitchen, with a profusion of

glazed tiles and local majolica plates both on the wall and in the cupboard on the side.

Main bedroom, which, as in the rest of the house, has white walls and a panelled wooden ceiling. The headboard of the bed is an antique relief of carved wood, over which there is a European painting in a baroque frame. It is worth noting the fireplace, which is outlined with an interesting stucco relief. On the mantelpiece there are several apothecary jars in blue glass and two Antigua majolica vases and on the wall above, the wooden torso of a Christ.

Above: *Detail of the dining room of another estate house, near Antigua. In the centre, a long table with rustic chairs, a folkloric tablecloth made up of several joined segments with an embroidered piece in the middle. A wooden cupboard of the second half of the nineteenth century. On the fireplace there are two Chinese-type ceramic plates and above it, the family shield sculpted in wood with gilding and polychrome. One can see part of the wooden beams of the roof with two opposite slopes, and an electric lamp that imitates a chandelier with candles.*

Opposite page: *View of the gallery of the same house, with a "Spanish terrace" roof supported by wooden pillars, without furniture and only adorned by flowerpots. The entrance floor is of clay tiles and its prolongation on the raised gallery is of wooden boards, with a wooden railing.*

Above: *In this corner of the house's study, painted masonry shelves display a beautiful collection of scent bottles and antique glass and ceramic pharmacist's jars. There is also a large framed Guatemalan textile and a colonial wooden bench, with cushions in a typical Guatemalan textile.*

Opposite page: *Contemporary vacation house in the countryside of a village near the city of Guatemala which incorporates traditional elements like wooden pillars with stone bases, stones in the arches of the door and balusters in the windows.*

Vestibule of the previous country house, from which one enters the dining room and main sitting room through a built-in stone arch. There is a sculpture

of San José on the table. In the corridor to the right, a colonial figure of a soul in purgatory, below which there is a wooden merry-go-round horse from a

village fair. To the right, a painting by the Salvadoran painter, Roberto Hueso.

View of the dining room of the same house. In the centre, a rustic waxed table; to the left, a side table on which there is a good display of Mayan vessels, and on the wall, a collection of traditional Antigua majolica plates. In the background, a painting by the Mexican artist, Rafael Coronel, below which there is a carved Mexican side table with two antique brass flower-vases. The atmosphere is complemented by the Turkish kilim rug in bright colours on the floor, the wooden ceiling, an antique gilded ornament beside the window and the electric lamp in the style of the old petroleum ones.

Large living room of the same house, made up of varied elements arranged in two joined living spaces. In the centre, the two facing sofas between which there are a kilim and a simple antique table which holds several small silver objects. In the background, a Peruvian painting by an unknown artist which represents the death of the Inca Atahualpa, flanked by two carved reliefs. Below this, there is a rustic table from Nahualá; to its left, a colonial wardrobe and other furniture and objects, like the amphora and the fragment of a Solomonic column, complete the decoration. In the space behind the wooden frame with columns, a large colonial oil painting. The wooden ceiling has two slopes.

Opposite page: *Modern country house on the outskirts of the capital. The pink living room is organized around two sofas upholstered in leather and textiles, with cushions in a folkloric fabric, and a centre table, decorated with popular wooden figures of animals and other objects. Above the large fireplace, whose wooden mantelpiece is decorated with jars of vitrified ceramic, there is a rustic carving of a two-headed eagle. The living room is complemented by a variety of furniture, small sculptures and objects of art.*

Above: *Sitting area of the bedroom of one of the houses that forms this estate of country homes. The arrangement is similar: two armchairs and a table in front of the fireplace, which is also decorated with popular pottery. On the walls there are two engravings and a wrought iron cross.*

Joined dining room and kitchen of the same country house. In this ample space we get an idea of the decorative tastes of the owner, who enjoys surrounding himself with diverse objects from the rich variety of popular art produced by craftsmen from different regions of Guatemala.

196

Opposite page: *Vacation house located in the upper part of northern Lake Atitlán, with an excellent view of the Tolimán and Atitlán volcanoes. Many vacation homes, in very diverse styles, have been built around this lake. To the left one sees the entrance area, with paved embankments and blue and yellow walls.*

Above: *Dining rooms of the house. In the foreground, the breakfast room, on a terrace beneath a canopy of canes and creepers; the rustic tables are painted in gay colours and the tableware is hand-painted Antigua ceramic. In the background one can see the formal dining room, with indigo walls.*

Interior setting of another contemporary vacation house on the shores of the Lake of Atitlán, with a rustic stone wall, floor of painted cement flagstones decorated with a rug from the region of Momostenango and indigenous textiles on the sofa. To the right, a wooden mortar and on the wall, a group of popular clay jugs and a painting by David Ordóñez. The ceiling is made of canes from the region.

Dining room of the same house, with a table made out of an old carved wooden door, surrounded by painted wicker chairs. The lamps are of gourds and the picture on the rustic stone wall is by David Ordóñez. To the right, on the sideboard, traditional ceramic angels from the region of Chinautla and in the background, a rustic wooden horse, an example of craftwork from the Nahaulá region.

Living room and dining room of a log cabin-type country house on the outskirts of Antigua. The natural colour of the walls contrasts with the dark green of the painted shelves and the fabric of the sofa and cushions. The decoration is noteworthy for the collection of wood and ceramic bird figures, especially cocks and hens, some drawn from the popular art of different countries and other contemporary ones inspired by Guatemalan traditions.

Living room of an artist's house in the city of Guatemala. In this exuberant mixture of colours and textures, painted wooden toys and majolica pieces are noteworthy. On the yellow wall in the background there is a painting by Magda Eunica Sánchez and on its left, an abstract oil painting by José Antonio Fernández. There are Art Deco armchairs behind a folkloric wooden table covered by colourful regional sashes. In the background, beside the window, a niche which displays various carved wooden saints, with articulated limbs (on hinges), in different sizes.

Bedroom of the same artist's
house in the city of Guatemala,
with a Guatemalan indigenous
cloth bedspread, covered by an
oriental textile, and a wooden

chest at the foot of the bed. In
the background, a folding chair
with an agave-fibre weave and to
the right, a fireplace with a niche
that displays a primitivist saint.

Above: *Another kind of vacation home, in the cattle-rearing region of El Progreso, which has a warm, dry climate. It is a simple thatched house with a palm-leaf roof built in the traditional way. Among its notable features are a gallery paved with round river stones, walls painted in yellow-ochre and, the only visible decoration, a popular crucifix.*

Opposite page: *Garden of the same farm, which in the photo on the right shows an attractive play of ponds, with the living area in the background surrounded by the tropical vegetation characteristic of the region.*

Above: *From the same thatched house, a terrace covered by a typical manaco-palm roof, furnished with sofas and armchairs upholstered in blue and white.*

Opposite page: *Living room with a display case that serves as a bar. The log-wood furniture, which copies the structure of the house, was made in the region and harmonizes with the place. On the yellow wall in the background there are an early painting by Erwin Guillermo and two by Salvador Galvez, both Guatemalan artists.*

Small sitting area betweeen the bedrooms. The furniture, also of logs, is highlighted by its typical Guatemalan fabrics. In the background, three terracotta candlesticks in the form of angels, from the village of Chinautla on the outskirts of the capital. On the left wall there are four pictures by the Guatemalan painter César Fortuny.

Main bedroom of the thatched cattle-farm house. On the board floor there is a rug woven in fibre and the log furniture is covered by typical Guatemalan textiles made by the designer, Geraldine de Caraman.

Pages 212-213: The same type of thatched house, on the banks of the river Tatín, near the gulf of the river Dulce. This architecture, typical of the region, harmonizes well with its setting.

Opposite page: *Another thatched vacation home, with a corozo-palm roof, on the banks of the river Tatín, designed by the decorator, John Heaton. The living room, which is of great luminosity and ventilation, with windows made of thin interwoven poles, is built around the masonry furniture decorated with cushions covered in typical Guatemalan textiles. The floor is of yellow-dyed cement with inlaid blue glazed tiles. The pictures are by the Mexican artist María Ruibalbo.*

Above: *Open area with a palm roof, from which hang hammocks woven in Antigua.*

Opposite page and above: *Two more views of the thatched house near the river Tatín, well adapted to the region, thanks to the designer's personal interpretation of traditional local building techniques. The second-storey bedroom, with a* *view of the river, is reached by the stairway in the centre. The bare furnishing consists of a mosquito net, an armchair, a little log table and a small woven indigenous rug. The floor is of wooden boards coloured by wax.*

Opposite page: *Terrace area of the same thatched house, with a view of the Río Tatín. Once again the armchairs are incorporated into the architecture and covered with a tapestry that utilizes Guatemalan textiles. The floor is of cement painted yellow and glazed tiles and the railing is of crossed stripped logs.*

Above: *Detail of a stairway with stone flowerbeds at its sides, in the midst of the region's exuberant vegetation. The ceramic tiles are combined with stairs of stone and glazed tiles.*

Opposite page: *Details of a contemporary house in the city of Guatemala, in which elements and ideas from the country's traditional architecture are used. An exterior gallery with a tiled roof and stone paving; a white-washed wall, without further decoration, except for the moulding, beneath which there are some niches for indirect light; and the fireplace with a semi-circular opening. In the background, a small sitting room with masonry seats built into the structure. On the floor there is a wooden mortar with its pestle, a trough and a clay pot, all of indigenous origin.*

Above: *Open space with vegetation and a stone floor, flowerbeds and flowers, which leads to an interior living room.*

221

Main sitting living room of the same residence in the city of Guatemala, which opens onto the patio-garden through large windows. Standing on several oriental rugs are pieces of simple contemporary furniture combined with traditional ones, all in a restrained white upholstery, with cushions made of kilims which lend a touch of colour. Several pre-Colombian Mayan vessels are on the central table, of contemporary design.

Another living room in the same house, with similar characteristics, including a floor of rustic granite stone, contemporary log-wood furniture covered in a rough white fabric and a centre table with a rounded marble surface. To the left, a mould to make cane sugar blocks, used as a candle-holder. The space is illuminated from the roof through a wooden grille. The red wall and plants strengthen its character.

Opposite page: *In the same residence in the city of Guatemala, a passage or corridor that connects the living rooms, with large windows and a fine parquet floor covered by oriental rugs. In the foreground, a seat made of rush and wood, with cushions covered in* kilims, *facing a wooden statue of a saint and a rustic chest.*

Above: *View of the main living room, which is divided by a contemporary central fireplace. On the wall in the background there are two paintings by the Nicaraguan painter Hugo Palma; beside the candles, a terracotta sculpture by the Guatemalan artist María Dolores Castellanos. The parquet floor is covered by a Persian rug.*

Living room of a contemporary house in the city of Guatemala, which is noteworthy for the decorative objects which create an atmosphere of baroque variety. To the left, a large picture, by the Yugoslavian painter Kristian Krékovic, of some Peruvian Indians; beside it, a small colonial oil painting with a gilded baroque frame and in the corner, a black and gold Solomonic column with an antique articulated sculpture seated on it. The wall in the background is divided by a fireplace, above which there is a large gilded artisanal mirror; on both sides of it there are shelves with pieces of blue and white ceramics mixed with pre-Hispanic figurines. Cushions of many colours are displayed on the furniture. On the tables, there are a multitude of small objects: sculptures, goldwork and, on the central one, a number of books.

Above: *Other details of the same residence. The white wall with a multitude of dance masks from the Guatemalan high plain showing the different figures used in diverse folkloric dances: personages of the Spanish conquest, Moors and Christians, the little bull, etc. Below them, a rustic carved wooden bench with gilded jaguar heads.*

Opposite page: *Bedroom with a sitting area, whose dominant element are the fabrics of the furniture and the curtains, which contrast with the yellow of the walls. The floor is of grey granite flagstones, with* dhurri *rugs from India. Above the fireplace is a picture by the Guatemalan artist, Miguel Angel Pérez, and two Guatemalan majolica plates.*

Opposite page: *Dining room painted in deep red, which does not diminish the full impact of the abundant collection of Antigua majolica and colonial paintings. On the left, the fireplace, beside which hang two gilded republican mirrors with their corresponding carved wooden console tables below. The two contemporary glass-topped tables rest on rustic wooden mortars placed on an oriental rug which is also red-toned. On the tables there are some Guatemalan colonial silver candlesticks.*

Above: *Another view of the same dining room. Moulded concrete shelves, gilded and shaped in the traditional manner, flank the door which leads to the kitchen. The collection of Antigua majolica pieces shows the wealth of this national craftsmanship.*

Bedroom of a contemporary house on the shores of the lake of Amatitlán, near the city of Guatemala, which combines the simplicity of the clay-tile floor, the beds of wrought iron with cane, the wooden roof beams and the austerely ornamented white walls.

The stairway of the same house
in Amatitlán, with elegant curves,
resting on large stones which form
a fountain. The skylights stand
out: a longitudinal one above the
window and the circular one in
the ceiling, which employs an old
cart wheel. The balustrade of the
stairway is of wrought iron with
a vegetal motif.

Above: *View of a
contemporary house on the
outskirts of the city of
Guatemala. A suspended
chimney with a baroque
polychrome angel divides the
corridor of one of the living
rooms that is illuminated by
large zenithal windows. The
house was designed by the
Guatemalan architect, Peter
Giesemann.*

Opposite page: *Large sitting
room of the same house, with
two levels and a parquet floor
covered by oriental rugs. Above
the fireplace, a colonial relief in
carved wood representing the
Virgin with the Apostles on the
Pentecost. The furnishing is
varied: a grand piano with
carved figurines, an oriental
screen and small tables, a centre
table of glass with a gilded
colonial support and diverse
decorative objects.*

Opposite page: *Sitting room of the same house. Here we can better see the size and shape of the large windows and the view of the trees on the outside, as well as the excellent Persian rug and the central table, which displays a colonial sculpture in polychromed wood. In the back, on the wardrobe, a figure by Maria Dolores Castellanos and a painting by the Guatemalan artist, Erwin Guillermo. One can also see an old merry-go-round horse in waxed wood on the rustic table.*

Above: *Terrace area open to the pool, beneath a cupola, with bamboo furniture and an antique wardrobe with two sculptures.*

Above: *Contemporary house in
the city of Guatemala. A raised
ceiling with a skylight, beneath
which there is a garden which
serves as a central sector that
arranges and connects the living
spaces of the social area. All
this allows for a good display
of the paintings and objects,
as well as setting off the display
case, open on both sides, in
which there are some Central
American pre-Hispanic pieces.*

Opposite page: *The spiral
staircase harmonizes the wood
of the floor, the stairs and the
ceiling - a modern atmosphere.
Architects Solares and Lara.*

Contemporary vacation home designed by the architect, José Asturias, with a view of the valley of Guatemala. The clever system of opening and closing the triangles allows the house to adapt itself to changing conditions of light and the needs of its inhabitants. Above, a small sitting room, with a fireplace in the centre and a kitchen with washbasin on the right, which can only be seen when the house is completely open. The fireplace and its base may be retracted when the occupants wish to.

240

The *bold placement of the house on the hillside, with an extraordinary view. Four sections open upwards to form the windows, and four go* downwards, as platforms or terraces. When closed, the house has an octahedral shape; it has two levels, with the sitting room, kitchen and dining room on the upper one and two bedrooms, a bathroom and an office in the lower one. When closed, it measures 36 sq. m.; with all modules opened, 112 sq.m

Pages 242-243: *Another view, which allows us to see the terrace of the house.*

BIBLIOGRAPHY

Above: *Garden built around the ruins of buildings destroyed by the earthquake of 1773 in the city of Antigua.*

Pages 246-247: *A stone-paved colonial street in the city of Antigua. In the background, the Acatenango and Fuego volcanoes.*

AGUIRRE CANTERO, Eduardo
1997 *Spaces and volumes. Contemporary architecture of Guatemala* Guatemala: Pisos El Águila.
ASTURIAS DE BARRIOS, Linda y Dina Fernández García
1992 *The history of Mayan dress and textiles.* Guatemala: Ediciones del Museo Ixchel.
ANNIS, Verle L.
1968 *The architecture of Antigua Guatemala 1543-1773* (Spanish-English bilingual edition). Guatemala: Editorial Universidad de San Carlos de Guatemala.
BERLIN, Heinrich
1952 *History of colonial religious art in Guatemala.* Guatemala: IDAEH.
1965 "Colonial artists and artisans in Guatemala. Notes for a catalogue". *Cuadernos de Antropología*, 5:5-35.
1988 *Essays on the History of Art in Guatemala and Mexico.* Publicación Especial 32. Guatemala: Academia de Geografía e Historia de Guatemala.
1983 y Jorge Luján Muñoz, *Burial mounds in Guatemala.* Guatemala: Academia de Geografía e Historia de Guatemala, 1983. Publicación Especial No. 25. 88 pp.
BERTRAND, Regis y Danielle Magne
1992 *The Textiles of Guatemala.* London: Studio Editions.

DUNN, Henry
1829 *Guatemala, or the Republic of Central America in 1827-8 being sketches and memorandums made during a twelve-months' residence.* London: James Nishet.
ESTERAS MARTÍN, Cristina
1994 *Silverwork in the Reino de Guatemala.* Guatemala: Fundación Albergue Hermano Pedro.
Galería Guatemala
1990 *A Selection of 20ᵗʰ Century Painting.* Volume 1. Guatemala: Grupo G&T.
1993 *Images of Gold.* Volume 2. Luis Luján Muñoz y Miguel Álvarez Arévalo. Guatemala: Corporación G&T.
1996 *Masterpieces. Heritage of the National Museum of Archaeology and Ethnology of Guatemala.* Volume 3. Guatemala: Corporación G&T.
1997 *Guatemala. Contemporary Art.* Guatemala: Fundación G&T.
General History of Guatemala
1993-1998 Jorge Luján Muñoz, General Director. 6 volumes
Guatemala: Asociación de Amigos del País-Fundación para la Cultura y el Desarrollo. References to architecture and art found in all the volumes, which deal with these subjects from the pre-Hispanic epoch to the present time.

JUÁREZ, Juan B.

1984 *The living painting of Guatemala.* Guatemala: without publisher.

LORENZANA DE LUJÁN, Irma y Luis Luján Muñoz

1987 *Notes on popular painting in Guatemala.* Guatemala: Programa Permanente de Cultura de la Organización Paiz.

LUJÁN MUÑOZ, Jorge

1974 "The architecture of Antigua, a monument of America". *Américas* (Washington, D.C.) 26, 5, S8-S13.

1978 *Some examples of urbanism in Guatemala in the late eighteenth century.* Guatemala: Sección Publicaciones, Facultad de Humanidades, 1978. 35 pp. (Lección Inaugural del Ciclo Académico 1978).

1985 "The first urban settlements in the Reino de Guatemala". *ASGHG*, 59:69-78.

1992 "2.1 Guatemala". En, *Historia Urbana de Iberoamérica.* Tomo III-2: *La Ciudad Ilustrada: análisis regionales (1750-1850).* Madrid: Quinto Centenario, Junta de Andalucía, Consejería de Obras y Transportes, Consejo Superior de Colegios de Arquitectos de España; pp. 415-433.

1996 "Architecture and building in the city of Guatemala at the end of the eighteenth century". *Revista de la Universidad del Valle de Guatemala,* No. 6 (diciembre), 12-24.

1997 "Guatemala:Colonial Architecture in the Reino de Guatemala". En, *Arquitectura Colonial Iberoamericana.* Graziano Gasparini, Coordinador. Caracas: Armitano Editores; pp. 145-178.

LUJÁN MUÑOZ, Luis

1972 *Synthesis of architecture in Guatemala* 2a. ed. Guatemala: Editorial Universitaria.

1975 *History of majolica in Guatemala.* Guatemala: Instituto de Antropología e Historia de Guatemala.

1977 *Fountains of Antigua Guatemala.* Guatemala: Consejo Nacional para la Protección de la Antigua Guatemala.

1987 *Masks and Moorish images in Guatemala.* Guatemala: Museo Popol Vuh, UFM.

MARKMAN, Sidney David

1966 *Colonial Architecture of Antigua Guatemala.* Memoirs. Vol. 64. Philadelphia: American Philosophical Society.

MILLA, José

1963 *Description of regional customs.* Third Edition. Biblioteca Guatemalteca de Cultura Popular No. 70. Guatemala: Ministerio de Educación Pública.

MONTGOMERY, George Washington

1839 *Narrative of a Journey to Guatemala, in Central America, in 1838.* New York.

MORELET, Arturo

1990 *Journey to Central America (Yucatan and Guatemala).* Serie Viajeros 2. Guatemala: Academia de Geografía e Historia.

Patronato de Bellas Artes de Guatemala

1995-1996 *A vision of contemporary art in Guatemala,* 3 volumes. Guatemala.

PETERSEN, Carmen L.

1976 *Maya of Guatemala. Life and Dress* (bilingual edition, English-Spanish). Guatemala: without publisher.

REINA, Rubén E. y Robert M. Hill II

1978 *The Traditional Pottery of Guatemala.* Austin University of Texas Press.

SCHEVILL, Margot Blum y Linda Asturias de Barrios

1997 *The Maya Textile Tradition.* New York: Harry N. Abrams.

YURRITA CUESTA, Alfonso

1967 *Housing in Antigua.* Architectural thesis. Universidad de San Carlos de Guatemala.